A TRUE BOOK™

National Parks
Hawai'i
Volcanoes

KARINA HAMALAINEN

Children's Press®
An Imprint of Scholastic Inc.

Content Consultant

James Gramann, PhD
Professor Emeritus, Department of Recreation, Park and Tourism Sciences
Texas A&M University, College Station, Texas

Library of Congress Cataloging-in-Publication Data

Names: Hamalainen, Karina. | Gramann, James H., consultant.
Title: Hawai'i volcanoes / by Karina Hamalainen ; content consultant, James
   Gramann, PhD, Professor Emeritus, Department of Recreation, Park and
   Tourism Sciences, Texas A&M University, College Station, Texas.
Description: New York, NY : Children's Press, [2019] | Series: A true book |
   Includes bibliographical references and index.
Identifiers: LCCN 2018032566| ISBN 9780531129333 (library binding) | ISBN
   9780531135020 (pbk.)
Subjects: LCSH: Hawaii Volcanoes National Park (Hawaii)--Juvenile literature.
   | Volcanoes--Hawaii--Juvenile literature.
Classification: LCC DU628.H33 H355 2019 | DDC 919.69/1--dc23

All rights reserved. Published in 2019 by Children's Press, an imprint of Scholastic Inc.
Printed in Heshan, China 62

Scholastic Inc., 557 Broadway, New York, NY 10012

1 2 3 4 5 6 7 8 9 10 R 28 27 26 25 24 23 22 21 20 19

**Front cover (main): Helicopter flying
by lava erupting from Kīlauea**

Front cover (inset): Boat near a lava waterfall

**Back cover: Kayaker near lava
entering the ocean**

Find the Truth!

Everything you are about to read is true *except* for one of the sentences on this page.

Which one is **TRUE**?

T or F Lava creates fertile soil for trees and other plants.

T or F Hawai'i Volcanoes National Park became a park soon after Hawai'i became a state.

Find the answers in this book.

Contents

THE **BIG** TRUTH!

Inside a Volcano

3 Amazing Animals

Kamehameha butterfly

A park ranger and visitors at a special lava viewing spot

4 A Fertile Land

What unique plants can be found in the park? . . . **29**

5 Protecting the Park

What will the park look like in the future? **35**

An offering to Pele

Lava flows out of Kīlauea's Puʻu ʻŌʻō Crater, one of the spots where lava escapes from the volcano.

Kīlauea means "spewing" in Hawaiian.

CHAPTER 1

Lava Rocks!

Hawai'i Volcanoes National Park

Earth's changes are usually slow. Wind and water reshape rocks. Land rises or falls. Continents shift. These changes can take millions of years. They are so gradual that humans don't notice them happening.

There are spots, however, where change is rapid and dramatic. Land is created and destroyed, forests burn away, cracks open in the earth. One such spot is Hawai'i Volcanoes National Park. With two of the world's most **active volcanoes**, this park is prone to sudden, violent change.

Hot Spots

Hawai'i Volcanoes National Park is on Hawai'i's Big Island. The state's land isn't just home to volcanoes. It's made by them! Under Earth's crust is a layer of hot melted rock, or **magma**. When magma bursts through the crust, it is called lava. Millions of years ago, magma began erupting from the seafloor. The lava collected and hardened, forming more than 130 islands and many volcanoes!

Timeline of a Hot History

400 CE
Polynesians discover the Hawaiian Islands.

1778
Captain James Cook lands on the Hawaiian island of Kaua'i. He and his crew are the first Europeans on the islands.

1835
American settlers start growing sugar on the islands. It becomes an important crop.

1898
Hawai'i becomes a U.S. territory.

The People of Hawai'i

About 1,600 years ago, people first arrived on the islands. They were sailors from Polynesia. Using the stars to navigate, they had traveled more than 2,000 miles (3,219 kilometers) in canoes. Much of Hawaiian culture is based on what these sailors brought with them. They brought animals and plants, such as taro—a potato-like vegetable—for food. They also brought music, dances, and other cultural elements.

1916

Hawai'i National Park (now Hawai'i Volcanoes National Park) becomes the country's 13th national park.

1959

Hawai'i becomes the 50th state.

1983

Kīlauea begins its most recent eruption. It hasn't stopped since.

2018

Kīlauea experiences new, violent eruptions. They cause destruction in and around the park.

Protecting the Volcanoes

Hawaiʻi's volcanoes have always fascinated people. Early Hawaiians visited Kīlauea to honor Pele (PAY-lay), the Goddess of Fire. They left her offerings of fruit, flowers, and other items. American and European settlers first saw Kīlauea's **caldera** in the 1820s. They wrote articles about it and other volcanoes, which drew more visitors.

Lorrin Thurston owned a newspaper in Honolulu, Hawaiʻi. He grew up exploring the volcanoes. In 1898, he proposed turning the area into a national park to protect the land and its wildlife. The park was created in 1916. That's before Hawaiʻi was even a state!

This park was the first national park created in a U.S. territory.

An offering to Pele, the Fire Goddess

National Park Fact File

A national park is land that is protected by the federal government. It is a place of importance to the United States because of its beauty, history, or value to scientists. The U.S. Congress creates a national park by passing a law. Here are some key facts about Hawai'i Volcanoes National Park.

Hawai'i Volcanoes National Park	
Location	Hawai'i
Year established	1916
Size	505 square miles (1,308 sq km)
Average number of visitors each year	Almost 2 million
Tallest feature	Mauna Loa summit: 13,679 feet (4,169 m)
Most recent eruption	Kīlauea: Nonstop since 1983 Mauna Loa: 1984
Erupting lava temperature	2,140°F (1,171°C)
Newest openings to erupt	In Kīlauea East Rift Zone, since May 2018

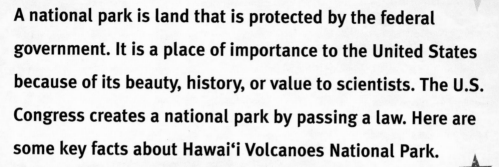

Hikers can walk across cooled, hardened lava.

An enormous volcano,
Mauna Loa's name
means "Long Mountain"
in Hawaiian.

CHAPTER 2

From Sea to Summit

Hawai'i Volcanoes National Park is the only national park in the state that goes from sea level to 13,679 feet (4,169 meters). That's the height of Mauna Loa's summit. It's the largest active volcano in the world! There is a cabin near the top of it. But any visitors to the cabin should be prepared to bundle up—sometimes it snows up there!

Despite being an active volcano, Mauna Loa often has snow on it in winter.

Fiery Summit

Kīlauea is the most active volcano in the world. It has been erupting nonstop since 1983! Sometimes, the eruption is explosive. At other times, the lava oozes steadily out of cracks. Depending on where the lava is coming out, it flows in different directions. Kīlauea's lava usually moves very slowly, giving people time to safely evacuate. But it still causes serious damage. In 2018, explosive eruptions destroyed homes and forests. Most of the park had to close.

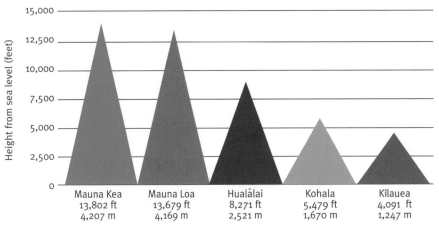

How Tall Are Hawai'i's Volcanoes?

Height from sea level (feet)

15,000 — 12,500 — 10,000 — 7,500 — 5,000 — 2,500 — 0

Mauna Kea	Mauna Loa	Hualālai	Kohala	Kīlauea
13,802 ft	13,679 ft	8,271 ft	5,479 ft	4,091 ft
4,207 m	4,169 m	2,521 m	1,670 m	1,247 m

NOTE: All volcanoes listed are considered active except Mauna Kea (dormant, or may erupt again) and Kohala (extinct, or does not erupt anymore).

Each day, Kīlauea spews enough lava to pave 20 miles (32 km) of a two-lane highway!

This 2005 photo shows a lake of lava once found in the Halema'uma'u Crater.

Studying Volcanoes

Near Kīlauea's summit is a caldera. Nestled inside is the Halema'uma'u Crater. During an eruption, steam and ash erupt from the crater. For many years, a lake of lava could be seen inside the crater. But during the 2018 eruption, the lava lake drained as lava flowed out of cracks in the volcano's side. The Hawaiian Volcano Observatory is there, too. Scientists there monitor the volcanoes for new eruptions.

Steamy . . . and Smelly

In some areas of the park, heat beneath the surface boils groundwater into steam. This steam escapes from the ground into the air at a spot called a **steam vent**. There's so much steam at Steaming Bluff that it looks like the meadow is on fire! This amazing site is near Kīlauea' summit.

Sulphur Banks is another nearby spot. *Pee-yoo!!* Here, the steam from the ground contains sulphur, a mineral that smells like rotten eggs. It also colors the rocks yellow.

Trees cannot grow near a steam vent. The ground is too hot for their roots.

Smelly steam fills the air at Sulphur Banks.

The Thurston Lava Tube is about 600 feet (183 m) long.

Tube Tour

The Thurston Lava Tube is an example of a formation sometimes created by volcanoes. Several hundred years ago, this long tube was formed by lava from the Kīlauea volcano. It acted like a pipe for hot lava from the volcano to flow through. When the eruption was over the tube was left behind. Lorrin Thurston, who helped create the park, discovered the lava tube in 1913.

Lots of Lava

Red-hot lava reaches the sea at Kamokuna Lava Delta. The delta is a fan-shaped area where new land forms from the fresh lava flowing from Kīlauea. At times, new pieces of land crumble into the ocean. Sometimes after a collapse, there's a waterfall of lava and rock. The extreme heat of the lava also boils ocean water into steam. The area is not always safe, and portions are at times closed to visitors.

As rocks hit the water in a lava waterfall, they can shoot more than 820 feet (250 m) in every direction!

Identifying Lava

New or old, red-hot or hardened, all lava in the park is one of two types: *pahoehoe* or *a'a*. Here's how to tell them apart.

	Pahoehoe	A'a
Speed of movement when lava is hot	Slow	Fast
Appearance	Goopy ripples with a smooth, shiny surface	Rocky and rough surface
Translation of name from Hawaiian	"Smooth, unbroken lava"	"Stony rough lava"
What it looks like		

Inside a Volcano

Earth is made up of four basic layers: the inner core, the outer core, the mantle, and the crust. Extreme pressure and heat deep inside the planet melts the rock into magma, which makes up part of the mantle. Magma can reach Earth's surface through a volcano. There are more than 1,500 active volcanoes on Earth. Check out how they erupt.

2 **GAS BUBBLES BUILD UP IN THE** magma. They cause the magma to push out of a volcano's vents, or openings. This is similar to what happens when you shake a bottle of soda, and then open the cap.

vent

lava

1 **SOME MAGMA RISES TO** Earth's crust. It collects in pools called magma chambers.

Earth's crust

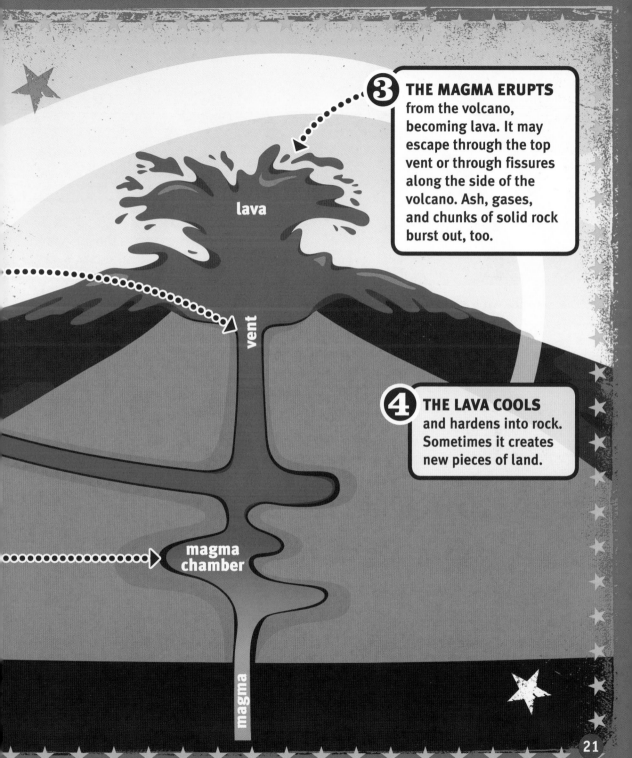

3 **THE MAGMA ERUPTS** from the volcano, becoming lava. It may escape through the top vent or through fissures along the side of the volcano. Ash, gases, and chunks of solid rock burst out, too.

lava

vent

4 **THE LAVA COOLS** and hardens into rock. Sometimes it creates new pieces of land.

magma chamber

magma

The Kamehameha butterfly is also known as the pulelehua.

CHAPTER 3

Amazing Animals

Hawai'i Volcanoes National Park is home to wildlife found nowhere else in the United States. That's because Hawai'i is so far from the mainland. Many of the animals native to the park have special adaptations specific for life on the islands.

Several park animals are symbols of Hawai'i. The Kamehameha butterfly is the state insect. The Hawaiian goose, or *nēnē*, is the state bird. And the state mammal is the Hawaiian monk seal.

 The Kamehameha butterfly is named after the family that ruled the Hawaiian Islands in the 1800s.

The 'apapane has the perfect beak for reaching into flowers.

Beautiful Beaks

The tweets and chirps of honeycreepers fill the park's forests. These birds are **endemic** to the island—they are found nowhere else in the world. Six species live in the park. The red *'apapane* is one with a short, curved beak for eating flower nectar. The yellow *'akiapōlā'au*'s scissorlike beak has a long, curved top and a shorter bottom. It scrapes at bark and plucks the spiders and caterpillars underneath. The brown *'akepa* uses its short beak to pry open seedpods in search of insects.

Saving the Nēnē

Nēnē are the world's rarest geese. Before humans arrived, more than 25,000 nēnē lived across Hawai'i. When people came, they hunted the geese. Settlers also introduced animals such as mongooses and cats that ate nēnē eggs and chicks. By 1952, only 30 nēnē were left. All of Hawai'i's other native geese were extinct. **Conservationists** began breeding nēnē to save the species in the 1960s. Today, there are more than 2,000 birds across the state.

Unlike its relative the Canada goose, the nēnē does not migrate when the seasons change and generally stays on land.

Sea Creatures

At the shore, a rare sight is the Hawaiian monk seal, the world's most endangered ocean mammal. The seals spend most of their time at sea, but also hang out on rocks in the sun. Farther out, spinner dolphins and humpback whales perform ocean acrobatics.

Green sea turtles and Hawaiian hawksbill turtles lay eggs on the park's beaches. Each nest has about 180 eggs. The eggs hatch at night, and the baby turtles crawl toward the sea.

The Hawaiian monk seal is one of only two species of monk seal on Earth.

Creepy Crawlers

Down in the soil and up among the leaves are hundreds of insects and spiders. In wet areas, the giant Hawaiian dragonfly flies through the air. With a wingspan of 6 inches (15 centimeters), it's the largest dragonfly in the United States. Resting on the leaves of koa trees are shimmering koa bugs. Even the barren-looking lava fields are home to crickets and wolf spiders searching for a meal.

Young koa bugs sit on the leaves of a native plant.

The koa bug is known as the "stinkless stinkbug." It is a kind of stinkbug, but it doesn't produce the smelly chemicals that others do.

The **Saddle Road** crosses the island of Hawai'i through lush, green fields to Mauna Loa.

A Fertile Land

The ash and lava from the park's volcanoes contain minerals that are very good for plants. As volcanic materials spread, they help create fertile soil. No wonder Hawai'i Volcanoes National Park has about 1,000 different plant species! Across the park's many **elevations,** from sea level to Mauna Loa's summit, are different types of forests. There are tropical rain forests, grasslands, scraggly **alpine** shrublands, and more. In the Ka'ū Desert, however, there are no plants at all!

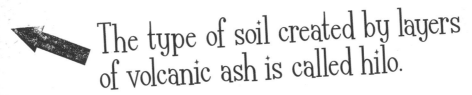

The type of soil created by layers of volcanic ash is called hilo.

The tall trees in the park's rain forest make people seem tiny!

Among the Trees

Rain forests are common at lower elevations. Tall koa and *'ohi'a lehua* trees tower from above. Long vines, orchids, and mosses hang from their branches. Ferns, grasses, and other green leafy plants cover the ground. There might be an occasional fern with red leaves along the trail. That's an *'ama'u* fern. Its new leaves are red. This fern can be found all over the park.

ʻOhiʻa Lehua in Danger

The park's most common tree is the ʻohiʻa lehua. In drier places, it is a small shrub. In the rain forest, it can grow as tall as 80 feet (24 m). It has bright-red flowers that look like puffballs.

A mysterious fungus is threatening these trees. The fungus prevents a tree's upper leaves from absorbing water. Without water, the tree dies. The ʻohiʻa lehua is an important species, and people are working to fight the fungus.

A flowering ʻohiʻa lehua plant grows out of cooled lava.

Mamane flower seeds are poisonous.

Elevated Plants

Above 6,000 feet (1,829 m), the air is cooler and drier. As a result, the plants there are smaller. The most common plant in Mauna Loa's alpine region is the *mamane*. This shrub has bright-yellow flowers and small, oval leaves. 'Ohi'a lehua grow here, too, but they are only 1 or 2 feet (30.5 or 61 cm) tall. Mauna Loa silverswords grow higher on the volcano. These large plants have a spiral of long, spiky leaves.

Pocket Forests

Lava is unpredictable. It mostly flows downhill, but it can take unexpected twists and turns. Some forests in its path go up in flames. But sometimes lava cuts around an area, creating an island of land surrounded by lava flows. These pocket forests are called *kīpuka*. There are many kīpuka on Mauna Loa's slopes. In one of these pocket forests, named Kīpukapuaulu, there are more native tree species per acre than anywhere else in the park!

The word *kīpuka*, which refers to a section of forest surrounded by lava, is a Hawaiian term meaning "opening."

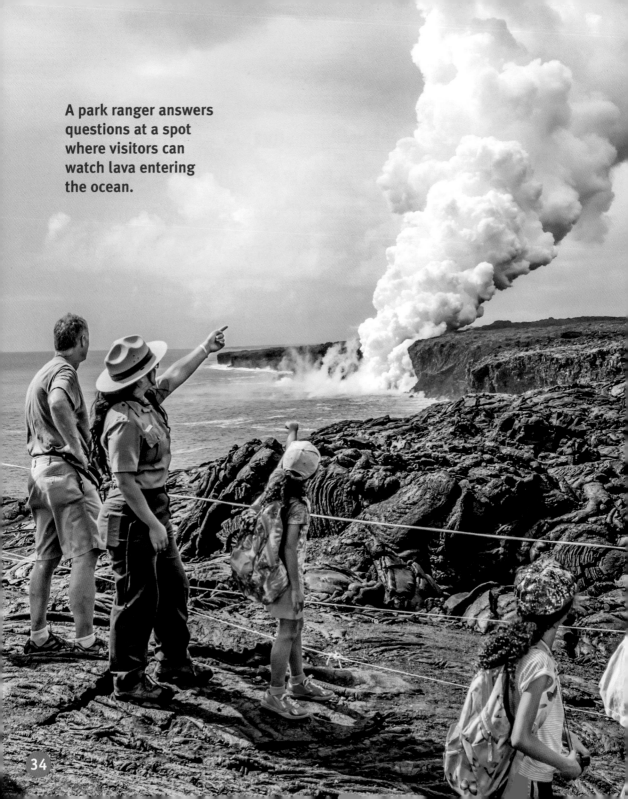

A park ranger answers questions at a spot where visitors can watch lava entering the ocean.

CHAPTER 5

Protecting the Park

Hawai'i Volcanoes National Park is unique. The park is also constantly changing, as eruptions create and destroy land. In addition, 54 endangered plant and animal species live here— the most in the National Park System. Many of these species could be harmed by volcanic ash and gases. Conservationists and park rangers are working hard to help them recover.

Hawai'i is home to eight national parks, with more than 6 million visitors total each year.

Island Invaders

The Hawaiian Islands are the planet's most isolated islands. The nearest continent is more than 2,300 miles (3,701 km) away. More than 90 percent of Hawai'i's plants and animals are endemic. When people bring creatures from elsewhere, it spells trouble for native species. The new arrivals are called **invasive species**. They cause damage and take space, food, and water that native species need.

The coqui, a kind of tree frog from Puerto Rico, has no natural predators in Hawai'i to keep its population from exploding.

Smoke rises along the coastline as lava enters the ocean.

Climate Concerns

Climate change is causing big problems for the park. That's because islands are sensitive to even small changes. Warming temperatures have caused sea levels to rise, which is increasing coastal **erosion**. Although volcanoes are adding land, other areas in the Hawaiian islands will be underwater as sea levels continue to rise. Rain patterns are also shifting. The average rainfall across Hawai'i has been decreasing over the past 100 years. These changes will affect the survival of native species.

Park rangers recommend all visitors wear sturdy shoes, long pants, hats, and sunscreen in the park.

A Changing Landscape

With two active volcanoes, the landscape of this park will always be changing. Fresh lava is creating more land and new islands. Pieces break off and fall into the sea. Sudden eruptions can turn forests into deserts. But even as the land changes, the park is there to protect the incredible volcanic features—new and old—and the plants and animals that live there. ★

Recent Eruption

Kīlauea has been oozing lava since 1983. Its most recent violent eruptions began in 2018. Earthquakes opened **fissures** along the side of the volcano, some through neighborhoods outside the park. People had to evacuate, and lava destroyed hundreds of homes. Large parts of the park had to be closed. Sulfur dioxide, a natural and poisonous gas, was released into the air. There are also other unpredictable dangers, including lava bombs, flying balls of red-hot lava. Experts do their best to track the eruption to keep people, plants, and animals safe.

The park averaged about 600 earthquakes each day during the 2018 volcanic activity at Kīlauea.

Map Mystery

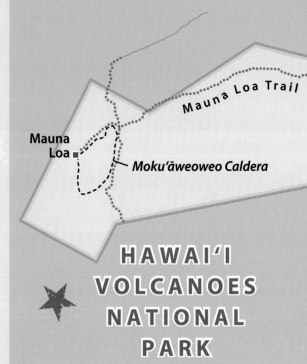

Mauna Loa ▪

Mauna Loa Trail

Mokuʻāweoweo Caldera

What hiking trail in Hawaiʻi Volcanoes National Park has a name that means "a fertile oasis of growing plants" in Hawaiian? Follow the directions below to find the answer.

HAWAIʻI VOLCANOES NATIONAL PARK

Directions

1. Start at the Puʻu Loa Petroglyphs at the southern end of the park. Here, the island's first residents carved images into the hardened lava.

2. Head north along Chain of Craters Road to Crater Rim Drive. Continue around the loop to Kīlauea Iki Crater.

3. Go northwest to see the Steam Vents and Sulphur Banks.

4. Then head west to the Mauna Loa Road. Almost there!

5. Follow the road north until you reach the first trail you see. What is its name?

HAWAI'I

Compass Rose
North
West   East
South

'Ohi'a Forest

11

Kīpukapuaulu Trail

Steam Vents & Sulphur Banks

Mauna Loa Road

Kīlauea Visitor Center

Jaggar Museum

Kīlauea Caldera

Thurston Lava Tube

Kīlauea Iki Crater

Pauahi Crater

Crater Rim Drive

Ka'ū Desert

Pu'u Huluhulu

Nāpau Crater

Mauna Ulu

Makaopuhi Crater

Hilina Pali Road

Mau Loa o Mauna Ulu

Chain of Craters Road

Hilina Pali

Pu'u Loa Petroglyphs

PACIFIC OCEAN

HAWAI'I

Area of map

Key
Paved roads
Hiking trails

Invasive Species Tracker!

Invasive species are a big problem in Hawai'i Volcanoes National Park. If you ever visit, keep an eye out for these plants and animals.

Fire tree
(Morella faya)

Where it's from: Canary Islands

When it arrived: 1800s

Why it's bad: It changes the soil and creates thick forests that crowd out other plants.

Kahili ginger
(Hedychium gardnerianum)

Where it's from: Himalaya Mountains of India, Nepal, and Bhutan

When it arrived: Unknown

Why it's bad: It carpets the forest floor so tree seeds can't take root.

Argentine ant
(Linepithema humile)

Where it's from: South America

When it arrived: 1940s

Why it's bad: It eats native insects that help native plants grow and thrive.

Small Asian mongoose
(Herpestes javanicus)

Where it's from: India

When it arrived: 1880s

Why it's bad: It eats small animals, as well as the eggs and hatchlings of endangered sea turtles.

Fountain grass
(Pennisetum setaceum)

Where it's from: Africa

When it arrived: 1880s

Why it's bad: It crowds out other plants and catches fire easily. It also reseeds quickly after a fire.

Feral pig *(Sus scrofa)*

Where it's from: Polynesia and Europe

When it arrived: 500s from Polynesia, 1700s from Europe

Why it's bad: It eats or destroys huge amounts of plants and makes it easier for invasive plants to grow and spread.

Number of volcanoes in the park: 2

Number of volcanoes on Hawai'i's Big Island: 5

Average temperature of Kīlauea's lava: 2,140°F (1,171°C)

Number of plant species in the park: About 1,000

Number of bird species: 62

Number of mammal species: 14, but only 2 are native to Hawai'i

Number of reptile and amphibian species: 15

Number of fish species: 4

Number of endangered plant and animal species: 54

Did you find the truth?

T Lava creates fertile soil for trees and other plants.

F Hawai'i Volcanoes National Park became a park soon after Hawai'i became a state.

Resources

Books

Flynn, Sarah Wassner, and Julie Beer. *National Parks Guide U.S.A.* Washington, DC: National Geographic, 2016.

Mattern, Joanne. *Hawai'i*. New York: Children's Press, 2018.

Meinking, Mary. *What's Great About Hawaii?* Minneapolis: Lerner Publications, 2016.

Squire, Ann O. *Volcanic Eruptions*. New York: Children's Press, 2016.

Woolf, Alex. *The Science of Natural Disasters: The Devastating Truth About Volcanoes, Earthquakes, and Tsunamis*. New York: Franklin Watts, 2018.

Visit this Scholastic website for more information on Hawai'i Volcanoes National Park:
★ www.factsfornow.scholastic.com
Enter the keywords **Hawaii Volcanoes**

Important Words

active volcanoes (AK-tiv vahl-KAY-nohz) volcanoes that have erupted at least once in the past 10,000 years and may erupt again

alpine (AL-pine) having to do with mountains

caldera (kal-DARE-uh) huge crater located at the site of a powerful volcanic eruption

conservationists (kahn-sur-VAY-shuhn-ists) people who work to protect valuable things

elevations (el-uh-VAY-shuhnz) heights above sea level

endemic (en-DEH-mik) native to one particular place and not found elsewhere in the world

erosion (ih-ROH-zhuhn) the wearing away of something by water or wind

fissures (FIH-shurz) long, deep, narrow openings in Earth's crust

invasive species (in-VAY-siv SPEE-sheez) species that are not native to a place and are causing damage

magma (MAG-muh) melted rock found beneath Earth's surface that becomes lava when it flows out of volcanoes

steam vent (STEEM VEHNT) an opening in Earth's surface from which steam and gases escape

territory (TER-ih-tor-ee) a region overseen by another country, such as the United States; people who live there are citizens of that country

Index

Page numbers in **bold** indicate illustrations.

About the Author

Karina Hamalainen has been a writer and editor of Scholastic's science and math magazines for nine years. Today, she is the associate editorial director of *Scholastic MATH* and *Scholastic ART* magazines. She's written stories about everything from the science of *Star Trek* to the effects of the *Deepwater Horizon* oil spill on the Gulf of Mexico. She lives in New York City, and tries to escape the city and explore the wilderness often!